Collins

Maths Progress Tests for White Rose

Year 5/P6

Rachel Axten-Higgs

William Collins' dream of knowledge for all began with the publication of his first book in 1819. A self-educated mill worker, he not only enriched millions of lives, but also founded a flourishing publishing house. Today, staying true to this spirit, Collins books are packed with inspiration, innovation and practical expertise. They place you at the centre of a world of possibility and give you exactly what you need to explore it.

Collins. Freedom to teach.

Collins
An imprint of HarperCollins*Publishers*
The News Building
1 London Bridge Street
London
SE1 9GF

MIX
Paper from
responsible sources
FSC® C007454

This book is produced from independently certified FSC™ paper to ensure responsible forest management.

For more information visit: **www.harpercollins.co.uk/green**

Browse the complete Collins catalogue at
www.collins.co.uk

British Library Cataloguing in Publication Data. A catalogue record for this publication is available from the British Library.

Author: Rachel Axten-Higgs
Publisher: Katie Sergeant
Commissioning Editor: Fiona Lazenby
Product Developer: Mike Appleton
Copyeditor: Gwynneth Drabble
Proofreader: Catherine Dakin
Design and Typesetting: Ken Vail Graphic Design
Cover Design: The Big Mountain Design
Production controller: Katharine Willard
Printed and bound by CPI Group (UK) Ltd, Croydon, CR0 4YY

Contents

How to use this book

Introduction

Collins Maths Progress Tests for White Rose have been designed to give you a consistent whole-school approach to teaching and assessing mathematics. Each photocopiable book covers the required mathematics objectives from the 2014 Primary English National Curriculum. For teachers in Scotland, the books can offer guidance and structure that is not provided in the Curriculum for Excellence Experiences and Outcomes or Benchmarks for Numeracy and Mathematics.

As stand-alone tests, the *Collins Maths Progress Tests for White Rose* provide a structured way to assess progress in arithmetic and reasoning skills, to help you identify areas for development, and to provide evidence towards expectations for each year group. Whilst the tests are independent of any textbook-based teaching and learning scheme to allow for maximum flexibility, the content for each test has been selected based on the suggested teaching order in the *White Rose Maths Schemes of Learning*, which are designed to support a mastery approach to teaching and learning.

Assessment of mathematical skills

At the end of KS1 and KS2, children sit tests to assess the standards they have reached in mathematics. This is done through national curriculum tests (SATs) in Arithmetic and Mathematical Reasoning. *Collins Maths Progress Tests for White Rose* have been designed to provide children with opportunities to explore a range of question types whilst building familiarity with the format, language and style of the SATs.

The Arithmetic tests comprise constructed response questions, presented as context-free calculations, to assess pupils' confidence with a range of mathematics operations as appropriate to the year group. Questions come from the Number, Ratio and Algebra domains.

The Reasoning tests present mathematical problems in a wide range of formats to ensure pupils can fully demonstrate mathematical fluency, mathematical problem solving and mathematical reasoning. They include both selected response questions (e.g. multiple choice, matching, yes/no) and constructed response questions. Questions may draw on all content domains and approximately half of the questions in the Reasoning tests are presented in context.

The tests follow the structure and format of SATs mathematics papers and are pitched at a level appropriate to age-related expectations for the year group. They provide increasing challenge within each year group and across the school, both in terms of content and cognitive demand, but also with increasing numbers of questions to build stamina and resilience. Using the progress tests with your classes at the end of each half-term should help pupils to develop and practise the necessary skills required to complete the national tests with confidence, as well as offering you a snapshot of their progress at those points throughout the year. You can use the results formatively to help identify gaps in knowledge and next teaching steps.

How to use this book

In this book, you will find twelve photocopiable tests: one arithmetic test and one reasoning test for use at the end of each half term of teaching. Each child will need a copy of the test. You will find Curriculum Content Coverage on page vi indicating the White Rose Scheme of Learning Block and associated Content Domain topics covered in each test across the year group. The specific Content Domain references indicating the year, strand and substrand, e.g. 2N1, for the questions in each test are in the tables on page 97. You may find it useful to make a photocopy of these tables for each child and highlight questions answered incorrectly to help identify any consistent areas of difficulty.

The number of marks available and suggested timing to be allowed are indicated for each test. The number of marks/questions in each test and the length of time allowed increases gradually across the year as summarised in the table below. Note that the Year 2 and Year 6 Summer term tests have been written as full practice papers assuming that all content will have been taught by this point. They mirror the number of marks and time allowed in the end of Key Stage 1 and end of Key Stage 2 test papers.

Year group	Test	Time allowed	Number of marks
5	Autumn 1 Arithmetic	25 minutes	30
5	Autumn 1 Reasoning	30 minutes	25
5	Autumn 2 Arithmetic	25 minutes	30
5	Autumn 2 Reasoning	30 minutes	25
5	Spring 1 Arithmetic	27 minutes	35
5	Spring 1 Reasoning	35 minutes	30
5	Spring 2 Arithmetic	27 minutes	35
5	Spring 2 Reasoning	35 minutes	30
5	Summer 1 Arithmetic	30 minutes	40
5	Summer 1 Reasoning	40 minutes	35
5	Summer 2 Arithmetic	30 minutes	40
5	Summer 2 Reasoning	40 minutes	35

To help you mark the tests, you will find mark schemes at the back of the book. These include the answer requirement, number of marks to be awarded, additional guidance on answers that should or should not be accepted and when to award marks for working in multi-mark questions.

Test demand

The tests have been written to assess progress in children's arithmetic and mathematical reasoning skills with the content and cognitive demand of questions increasing within each book and across the series to build towards to end of key stage expectations of the SATs. Since the national tests may cover content from the whole key stage, each progress test contains some questions which draw on content from earlier terms or previous year objectives (particularly in autumn term tests). This ensures that prior content and skills are revisited.

The level of demand for each question has been provided within the mark schemes for each test using the notation T (working towards), E (expected standard) or G (greater depth). These ratings are given as an indication of the level of complexity of each question taking into account the thinking skills required to understand what is being asked, the computational complexity in calculating the answer, spatial reasoning or data interpretation required and the response strategy for the question.

Performance thresholds

The table below provides guidance for assessing how children perform in the tests. Most children should achieve scores at or above the expected standard, with some children working at greater depth and exceeding expectations for their year group. While the thresholds bands do not represent standardised scores, as in the end of key stage SATs, they will give an indication of how pupils are performing against the expected standards for their year group. The thresholds have been set broadly assuming that pupils who achieve greater than 60% will be working at the expected standard and those who

score more than 80% are likely to be working at greater depth. However, pupils will all have individual strengths and weaknesses, so it is possible that they could be working towards the expected standard in some areas but at greater depth in others. For this reason, using the content domain coverage tables to identify common areas of difficulty alongside your own professional judgement, will enable you to identify pupils' specific gaps in knowledge and areas where further teaching may be required.

Tracking progress

A record sheet is provided to help you illustrate to children the areas in which their arithmetic and reasoning skills are strong and where they need to develop. A spreadsheet tracker is also provided via collins.co.uk/assessment/downloads which enables you to identify whole-class patterns of attainment. This can be used to inform your next teaching and learning steps.

Editable download

All the files are available online in Word and PDF format. Go to collins.co.uk/assessment/downloads to find instructions on how to download. The files are password protected and the password clue is included on the website. You will need to use the clue to locate the password in your book.

You can use these editable files to help you meet the specific needs of your class, whether that be by increasing or decreasing the challenge, by reducing the number of questions, by providing more space for answers or increasing the size of text for specific children.

Year group	Test	Working towards (T)	Expected standard (E)	Greater depth (G)
5	Autumn 1 Arithmetic	17 marks or below	18–23 marks	24–30 marks
5	Autumn 1 Reasoning	14 marks or below	15–19 marks	20–25 marks
5	Autumn 2 Arithmetic	17 marks or below	18–23 marks	24–30 marks
5	Autumn 2 Reasoning	14 marks or below	15–19 marks	20–25 marks
5	Spring 1 Arithmetic	20 marks or below	21–27 marks	28–35 marks
5	Spring 1 Reasoning	17 marks or below	18–23 marks	24–30 marks
5	Spring 2 Arithmetic	20 marks or below	21–27 marks	28–35 marks
5	Spring 2 Reasoning	17 marks or below	18–23 marks	24–30 marks
5	Summer 1 Arithmetic	23 marks or below	24–31 marks	32–40 marks
5	Summer 1 Reasoning	20 marks or below	21–27 marks	28–35 marks
5	Summer 2 Arithmetic	23 marks or below	24–31 marks	32–40 marks
5	Summer 2 Reasoning	20 marks or below	21–27 marks	28–35 marks

Curriculum content coverage

All content objectives from the Year 5 National Curriculum Programme of Study for Mathematics are covered within one or more of the half-termly progress tests across the year. The content for each test is based on the suggested teaching order of the White Rose Maths Schemes of Learning. The table below shows from which teaching blocks the content for each test is drawn. Where the White Rose Maths blocks are devoted to skills or consolidation rather than introduction of new content, these blocks are not covered by the tests. The Summer tests for Year 5 draw on content from previous blocks.

White Rose Schemes of Learning blocks			Autumn 1: Arithmetic	Autumn 1: Reasoning	Autumn 2: Arithmetic	Autumn 2: Reasoning	Spring 1: Arithmetic	Spring 1: Reasoning	Spring 2: Arithmetic	Spring 2: Reasoning	Summer 1: Arithmetic	Summer 1: Reasoning	Summer 2: Arithmetic	Summer 2: Reasoning
Blocks	Weeks	Topics												
Autumn Block 1	Weeks 1–3	Number: Place Value	✔	✔							✔	✔	✔	✔
Autumn Block 2	Weeks 4–5	Number: Addition and Subtraction	✔	✔	✔						✔	✔	✔	✔
Autumn Block 3	Weeks 6–7	Statistics		✔		✔						✔		✔
Autumn Block 4	Weeks 8–9	Number: Multiplication and Division			✔	✔					✔	✔	✔	✔
Autumn Block 5	Weeks 10–11	Measurement: Perimeter and Area				✔						✔		✔
Autumn Block 6	Week 12	Consolidation												
Spring Block 1	Weeks 1–3	Number: Multiplication and Division					✔	✔			✔	✔	✔	✔
Spring Block 2	Weeks 4–9	Number: Fractions					✔	✔	✔	✔	✔	✔	✔	✔
Spring Block 3	Weeks 10–11	Number: Decimals and Percentages							✔	✔	✔	✔	✔	✔
Spring Block 4	Week 12	Consolidation												
Summer Block 1	Weeks 1–4	Number: Decimals									✔	✔	✔	✔
Summer Block 2	Weeks 5–7	Geometry: Properties of Shape										✔		✔
Summer Block 3	Week 8	Geometry: Position and Direction												✔
Summer Block 4	Weeks 9–10	Measurement: Converting units												✔
Summer Block 5	Week 11	Measurement: Volume and Capacity												✔
Summer Block 6	Week 12	Consolidation												

Collins Maths Progress Tests for White Rose

Year 5 Autumn Half Term 1: Arithmetic

Name _____

1 | 895 − 100 =

1 mark

2 | 609 + 76 =

1 mark

3 | 954 − 187 =

1 mark

4 | 7,487 − 999 = ☐

1 mark

5 | 132 ÷ 12 =

1 mark

6 | ☐ = 3,967 + 638

1 mark

Name _____

7 $8,096 - 1,000 =$

1 mark

8 $854 \div 1 =$

1 mark

9 $19 - 25 =$

1 mark

10 $9 \times 8 =$

1 mark

11 $4 \times 7 \times 3 =$

1 mark

12 $90 \times 100 =$

1 mark

Name _____

13 $3,467 + 5,976 =$

1 mark

14 $90 \times 50 =$

1 mark

15 $6^2 + 10 =$

1 mark

16 $XII + VIII =$

1 mark

17 $8,705 - 6,854 =$

1 mark

18 $4,200 \div 70 =$

1 mark

19 $5^2 + 20 =$

1 mark

20 $8{,}704 - 2{,}967 =$

1 mark

21 $8^3 - 50 =$

1 mark

22 $360 \div 6 =$

1 mark

23 $9{,}800 \div 100 =$

1 mark

24 $1.98 \times 100 =$

1 mark

25 6,008 + 2,996 =

1 mark

26 CCC + D =

1 mark

27 24.98 ÷ 10 =

1 mark

28 [   ] = 300,000 + 60,000 + 500 + 4

1 mark

29 890,906 = 800,000 + [   ] + 900 + 6

1 mark

30 904,768 = [   ] + 4,000 + 700 + 60 + 8

1 mark

Total marks ………/30

1   Write the three missing digits to make this **addition** correct.

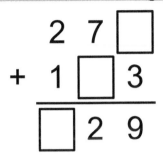

2 marks

2   Write the missing number.

One is done for you.

450	is 100 less than	550
	is 100 less than	990

1 mark

3   Tamzin completes this calculation.

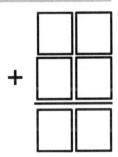

Write an **addition** calculation, using the numbers above, she could use to check her answer.

1 mark

4 This table shows the number of people in a city who play different sports.

Sport	Number
Football	3,698
Rugby	4,096
Netball	4,121
Hockey	3,067
Tennis	1,987

a) What is the **total** number of people taking part in Rugby and Hockey?

people

1 mark

b) What is the **difference** between the numbers of people taking part in Netball and Tennis?

people

1 mark

5 Complete this table with the missing numbers.

One row has been done for you.

Number	1,000 more
1,125	2,125
64	
	4,876
26,756	

2 marks

6 Asif thinks of a **whole** number.
He multiples it by 5.
He rounds his answer to the nearest 10.
The result is 120.

Write **all** the possible numbers that Asif could have started with.

2 marks

7 754,987

Complete the boxes in the table using the number above. One has been done for you.

Round to the…	Answer
nearest 10…	754,990
nearest 100…	
nearest 1,000…	
nearest 10,000…	
nearest 100,000…	

3 marks

8 Harry has taken the temperature in the morning for every day in December.
The highest temperature he has recorded is 16.5°C.
The lowest temperature he has recorded is −7.5°C.

What is the difference between these two temperatures?

	°C

1 mark

9 3,894,752

Complete the boxes below using the number above.

The number has:

| hundred thousands |

| thousands |

| tens |

2 marks

10 Here is a number written in Roman numerals.

C L I

Write the number in figures.

| |

1 mark

11 This table shows the populations of five towns.

Town	Population
Alphaton	530,375
Betastock	616,430
Castleby	726,939
Deltaside	612,490
Epsworth	587,956

Put these towns in order of population, starting with the lowest population.

lowest

1 mark

12 Here is part of a bus timetable from Exenfort to Hamsford.

Exenfort	15.03	15.43	16.15	16.49
Tintenville	15.14	15.54	16.26	17.00
Samsgood	15.45	16.25	16.57	17.31
Littleford	16.12	16.52	17.24	17.58
Hamsford	16.40	17.20	17.52	18.26

a) How many minutes does it take the 15.43 bus to go from Exenfort to Hamsford?

minutes

1 mark

Samuel arrives at Samsgood at 16.45.

b) What is the **earliest** time he can reach Littleford on the train?

1 mark

13 This graph shows a remote control helicopter's height at different times.

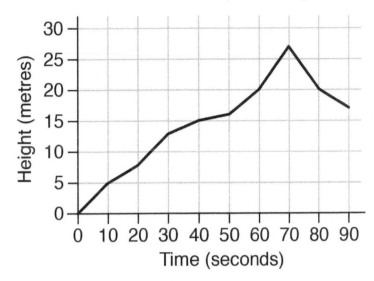

Answer the questions below.

a) What was the helicopter's height at 50 seconds?

| metres |

1 mark

b) How long did it take for the helicopter to rise from 5 metres to 15 metres?

| seconds |

1 mark

14 Sophie and Sebastian have each saved their pocket money.
Sophie has £76.87.
Sebastian has 112.67.

a) 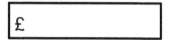 How much money do they have altogether?

£ _____

1 mark

Sophie buys something for £56.98.
Sebastian spends £69.65.

b) How much more does Sebastian spend than Sophie?

Show your method

£ _____

2 marks

Total marks ………/25

Name _____

1   54 + 298 =

1 mark

2   875 + 10 =

1 mark

3   608 − 10 =

1 mark

4   6,709 − 1,598 =

1 mark

5   78 + 1,000 =

1 mark

6   7,543 + 932 =

1 mark

7   63 + 49 =

1 mark

8   9,003 − 6,978 =

1 mark

9   9,876 − 1,000 =

1 mark

10   18 + 36 =

1 mark

11   XIX − VII =

1 mark

12   16 − 24 =

1 mark

Name _____

13 $408,084 - 90 =$

1 mark

14 $-19 + 24 =$

1 mark

15 $58,903 + 6,893 =$

1 mark

16 $IV + IX =$

1 mark

17 $798,578 + 50 =$

1 mark

18 $-10 + 27 =$

1 mark

19 VII + VIII =

1 mark

20 40 − 50 =

1 mark

21 8 − 17 =

1 mark

22 4,567 + 7,378 =

1 mark

23 1,986,409 − 98,600 =

1 mark

24 278,376 − 76,498 =

1 mark

25 789,548 − 96,059 =

1 mark

26 8,947 = 8,000 + [   ] + 40 + 7

1 mark

27 1,000 + 700 + [   ] = 1,760

1 mark

28   [   ] + 60,000 + 5,000 + 80 = 865,080

1 mark

29   970,780 = 900,000 + [   ] + 700 + 80

1 mark

30   931,070 = 900,000 + 30,000 + [   ] + 70

1 mark

Total marks ………/30

1 Joshua has ordered 12 tricycles for his shop.

How many wheels does he have on the 12 tricycles?

| | wheels |

1 mark

2 Here is a bar chart showing the number of children in a class who own each of the pets shown.

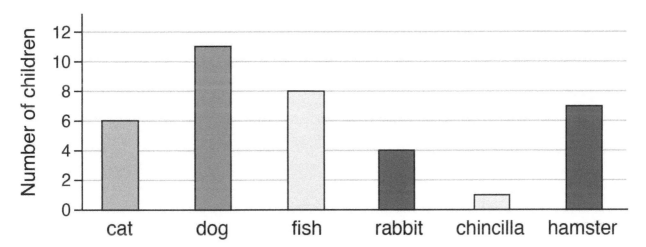

Answer the questions about the bar chart.

a) How many more children own dogs than rabbits?

| |

b) How many more children own hamsters than chincillas?

| |

c) How many children own pets altogether?

| |

2 marks

3 Graham buys 9 packs of multipack snacks. There are 18 packets of snacks in each pack.

How many packets of snacks has he bought altogether?

Show your method

packets

2 marks

4 Here is a rectilinear shape drawn on a 1cm^2 grid.

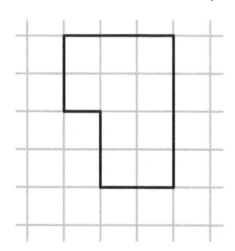

What is the area of the shape?

cm^2

1 mark

5 Here is a tally chart showing the hair colour of children in Class 5.

Hair colour	Number
brown	卌 卌 卌 I
black	卌
blonde	卌 II
red	II

a) How many children have blonde hair?

```

```

1 mark

b) How many more children have brown hair than black hair?

```

```

1 mark

c) What is the difference between the most and least common hair colour?

```

```

1 mark

6 In a school, there are 364 children.
Each child is given a set of 10 crayons.

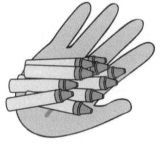

How many crayons are needed altogether?

```

```

1 mark

7 Sebastian is completing factor boards. He has got stuck and only completed three numbers.

Complete the factor board for the number 36.

36
1
3
18

3 marks

21

8   Here is a school timetable.

	9.00 – 10.00		10.20 – 11.20	11.20 – 12.20		1.30 – 2.30	2.30 – 3.30
Monday	English		Maths	Art		History	RE
Tuesday	Maths		English	Dance		PE	Geography
Wednesday	Maths	BREAK	Science	English	LUNCH	Music	Science
Thursday	English		Swimming	Maths		Drama	Art
Friday	Maths		English	Music		PE	

a) What lesson is at 10.20 on a Wednesday?

1 mark

b) How long is lunchtime?

minutes

1 mark

c) How much time is spent doing English in a week?

hours

1 mark

d) What day and time is swimming?

1 mark

9   Chris packs jars into boxes so they look like this:

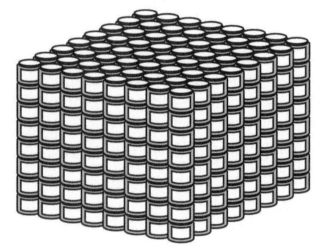

a) Circle the correct notation to show this:

    8^3 8^2 $8 \times 8 \times 8 \times 8$ 8^4

1 mark

b) How many jars are in one box?

jars

1 mark

Name _____

10 Andrea needs to calculate the perimeter of her garden so she can buy a fence.

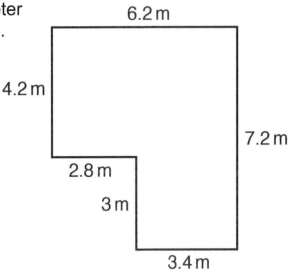

Calculate the **perimeter** of the garden.

Show your method

m

2 marks

11 Coaches hold 58 passengers. A school needs to take all of its 667 children and staff to the theatre by coach.

How many coaches do they need to use to transport **everyone** to the theatre?

Show your method

coaches

3 marks

12 Marcus is buying new turf for this playground:

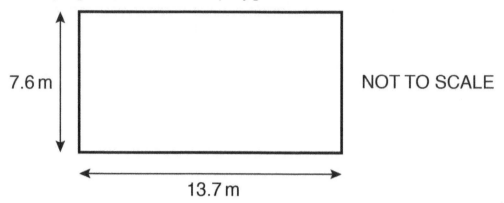

7.6 m

13.7 m

NOT TO SCALE

Calculate the area of the playground.

Show your method

m²

1 mark

Total marks ..../25

1 $56 \times 4 =$

1 mark

2 $\dfrac{2}{7} + \dfrac{3}{7} =$

1 mark

3 $435 + 389 =$

1 mark

4 $245 \times 5 =$

1 mark

5 $\dfrac{5}{8} + \dfrac{7}{8} =$

1 mark

6 $9 \times 4 \times 7 =$

1 mark

7 $737 \times 6 =$

1 mark

8 $2\frac{5}{9} - \frac{13}{9} =$

1 mark

9 $108 \div 9 =$

1 mark

10 $XL - XI =$

1 mark

11 $792 + 10 =$

1 mark

12 $\frac{5}{6} + \frac{1}{12} =$

1 mark

13 −25 + 60 =

1 mark

14 $\frac{7}{8}$ of 40 =

1 mark

15 1,967 + 698 =

1 mark

16 6,300 ÷ 7 =

1 mark

17 $\frac{3}{5} - \frac{1}{3} =$

1 mark

18 986 ÷ 100 =

1 mark

19 $7^3 + 27 =$

1 mark

20 $70 \times 700 =$

1 mark

21 DCCC + CC =

1 mark

22 $4{,}986 + 2{,}965 =$

1 mark

23 $\dfrac{5}{6} \times 4 =$

1 mark

24 $7.98 \times 10 =$

1 mark

25 $8^2 - 15 =$

1 mark

26 $9.08 \times 10 =$

1 mark

27 $\frac{15}{7} \times 6 =$

1 mark

28 $56,000 \div 70 =$

1 mark

29 $8,954 - 4,087 =$

1 mark

30 $\frac{12}{7} + \frac{13}{28} =$

1 mark

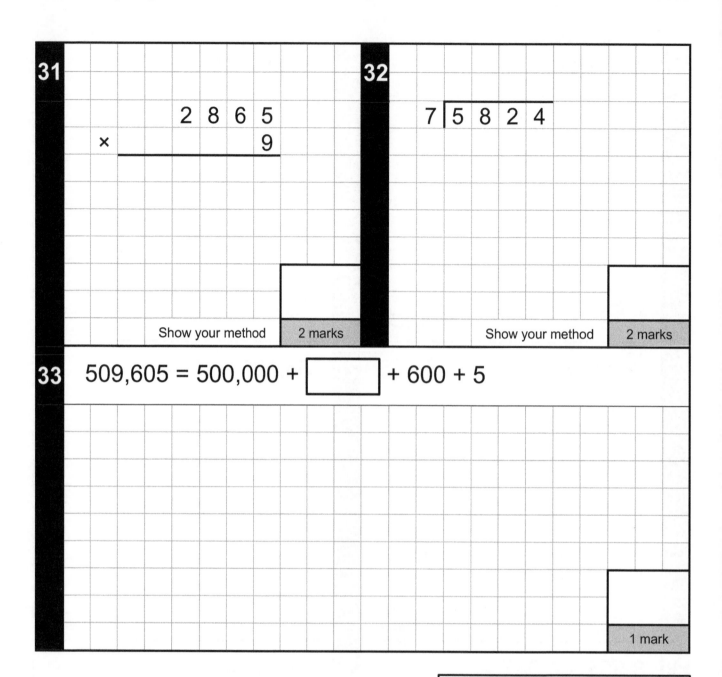

31

$$\begin{array}{r} 2\ 8\ 6\ 5 \\ \times \qquad 9 \\ \hline \end{array}$$

Show your method   2 marks

32

$$7\overline{)5\ 8\ 2\ 4}$$

Show your method   2 marks

33   509,605 = 500,000 + ☐ + 600 + 5

1 mark

Total marks ………/35

1 Sabina has 6 dogs and 3 cats.
Each animal has 4 legs.

How many legs are there altogether?

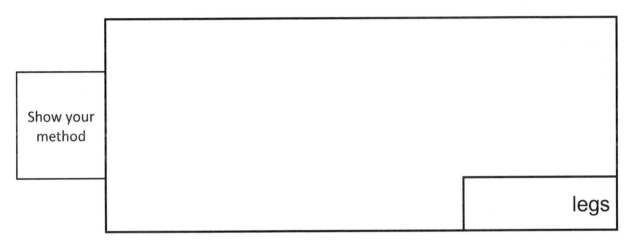

Show your method

legs

1 mark

2 A group of friends order some takeaway food that costs £63.
They share the cost **equally**.
They each pay £7.

How many friends are in the group?

friends

1 mark

3   Match each shape to its equivalent fraction.

                    $\frac{1}{2}$

                    $\frac{9}{16}$

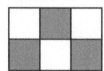 $\frac{1}{4}$

                    $\frac{3}{4}$

                    $\frac{1}{3}$

2 marks

4   Tick the two numbers that are equivalent to $\frac{3}{4}$.

Tick two

0.25

0.75

$\frac{75}{100}$

$\frac{80}{100}$

$\frac{3}{7}$

1 mark

5 $78 \div \boxed{} = 0.78$

1 mark

6   Complete the fractions to make two equivalent fractions.

$\dfrac{\boxed{}}{5} = \dfrac{8}{10} = \dfrac{56}{\boxed{}}$

2 marks

7 Sharon says, ' $\frac{20}{8}$ is the same as $2\frac{1}{2}$ '.

Is she correct?   Y / N

Explain your answer.

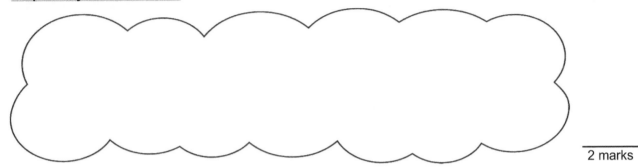

2 marks

8 Eliza makes two cakes for a fair.
1 cake is cut into 12 slices and she sells 7 slices.
1 cake is cut into 8 slices and she sells 6 slices.

What fraction of a cake does she have left in total?

Show your method

2 marks

9 Chad shares a pizza with his friend every Friday.

He eats $\frac{5}{8}$ of the pizza every Friday for 13 weeks.

How much pizza does he eat altogether as a mixed number?

Show your method

pizzas

2 marks

10 Here are some fractions.

Match each fraction to its decimal equivalent.

One has been done for you.

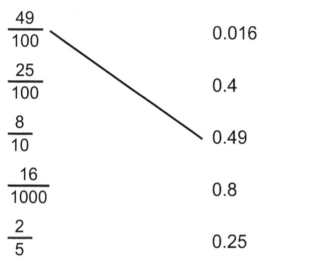

$\frac{49}{100}$ 0.016

$\frac{25}{100}$ 0.4

$\frac{8}{10}$ 0.49

$\frac{16}{1000}$ 0.8

$\frac{2}{5}$ 0.25

_____
2 marks

11 Freya decided to wash cars in the summer holidays.
For every car she washed, she was paid £3.
For every van she washed, she was paid £5.

Freya washes 68 cars and a small number of vans. She earns £234 in total.
How many vans did she wash?

Show your
method

vans

_____
2 marks

12 At the end of a film, the year is
given in Roman numerals.

Write the year MMXVIII in figures.

_____

_____
1 mark

13 Mr Sanjay collected 378 eggs from his chicken farm one morning.
He needs:
6 boxes of 15 eggs
7 boxes of 12 eggs
The rest need to go into boxes of 6.

How many boxes of 6 eggs does he make?

Show your
method

boxes

3 marks

14 Here are four fraction cards.

$$\frac{1}{2} \quad \frac{1}{5} \quad \frac{1}{4} \quad \frac{9}{10}$$

Use any three cards to make this correct.

☐ < ☐ < ☐

1 mark

15 Write the two missing digits to make
this **long multiplication** correct.

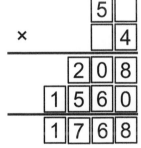

```
      5 ☐
  ×   ☐ 4
  ─────────
    2 0 8
  1 5 6 0
  ─────────
  1 7 6 8
```

Show your
method

3 marks

35

16 A chocolate factory produces 993 white chocolates.
They package these into 43 boxes with an equal number in each box.

a) How many chocolates are in each box?

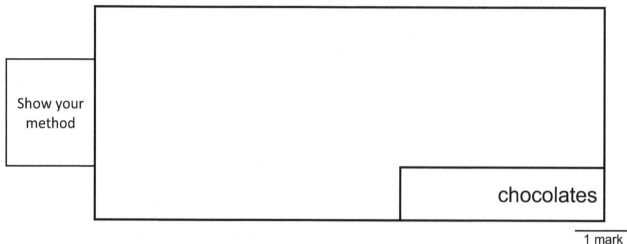

Show your method

chocolates

1 mark

b) How many chocolates are left over?

chocolates

1 mark

17 Round 95,365

a) to the nearest 10

1 mark

b) to the nearest 1,000

1 mark

Total marks ..../30

Name _____

1   687 − 193 =

1 mark

2 $\frac{1}{3} + \frac{2}{9} =$

1 mark

3   276 + 877 =

1 mark

4   8,679 + 1,000 =

1 mark

5   547 × 8 =

1 mark

6 $\frac{4}{10} = \frac{}{100}$

1 mark

7 3.6 + 0.08 =

1 mark

8 $\frac{3}{4} - \frac{1}{3} =$

1 mark

9 $\frac{1}{4} = 0.\boxed{}$

1 mark

10 1.9 + 1.06 =

1 mark

11 £1.78 + £17.58 =

1 mark

12 37,867 − 21,067 =

1 mark

13 387 − 487 =

1 mark

14 $\frac{3}{4}$ = ☐ %

1 mark

15 0.86 = $\frac{}{100}$

1 mark

16 $\frac{3}{7} + \frac{5}{7}$ =

1 mark

17 4 − 3.876 =

1 mark

18 $\frac{1}{2} + \frac{3}{5}$ =

1 mark

Name _____

19 $\frac{2}{9} = \frac{}{36}$

1 mark

20 $17.3 - 9.76 =$

1 mark

21 $\frac{54}{1000} = 0.\boxed{}$

1 mark

22 $\frac{3}{7}$ of $63 =$

1 mark

23 $30\% = \frac{}{10}$

1 mark

24 $0.54 = \frac{54}{}$

1 mark

25 $\dfrac{4}{7} = \dfrac{}{56}$

1 mark

26 $1\dfrac{3}{4} + \dfrac{3}{4} =$

1 mark

27 $\dfrac{5}{6} - \dfrac{3}{10} =$

1 mark

28 $56.9 + 27.46 =$

1 mark

29 $5^3 + 17.56 =$

1 mark

30 $2\dfrac{1}{6} \times 8 =$

1 mark

31 $\frac{3}{5} + \frac{2}{3} =$

1 mark

32

$$\begin{array}{r} 3\ 5\ 6\ 7 \\ \times \quad\quad 1\ 2 \\ \hline \end{array}$$

Show your method   2 marks

33

$6\,|\,8\ 0\ 4\ 3$

Show your method   2 marks

Total marks ..../35

1 Circle the number that is **100 times** greater than seven hundred and six.

706   70,600   7,060   706,000   760

_____
1 mark

2 Samira buys 3 large sheets of stickers and 5 small sheets of stickers.
Each large sheet has 52 stickers.
Each small sheet has 30 stickers.

How many stickers did Samira buy altogether?

Show your method

stickers

_____
2 marks

3 Sofia uses these digit cards.

4 7 9

She makes a 2-digit number and a 1-digit number.
She multiples them together.
Her answer is a multiple of 6.

What could Sofia's multiplication be?

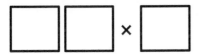

☐☐ × ☐

_____
1 mark

4   These diagrams show three equivalent fractions.

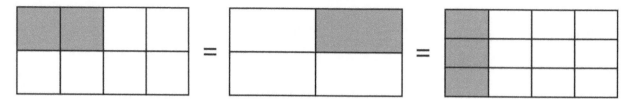

Write the missing values.

$$\frac{\boxed{}}{8} = \frac{1}{4} = \frac{3}{\boxed{}}$$

1 mark

5   A race is 2,500 km long.

Joel has completed $\frac{2}{5}$ of the race.

How many km are **left** for Joel to run?

Show your method

km

2 marks

6   Manu had £18.65 in her money box.
She spent £7.15 on a new toy.
She spent £2.95 on a present for her brother.

Work out the amount she has left in her money box.

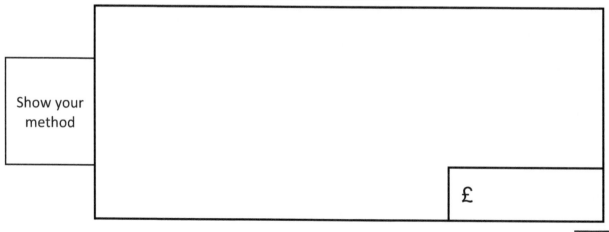

Show your method

£

2 marks

7 Circle the improper fraction that is equivalent to $5\frac{7}{9}$.

$\frac{35}{9}$ $\frac{52}{9}$ $\frac{50}{9}$ $\frac{57}{9}$ $\frac{60}{9}$

_____
1 mark

8 Write these numbers in order of size, starting with the **smallest**.

2.8   0.54   2.08   0.687

[ ]   [ ]   [ ]   [ ]

smallest

_____
1 mark

9 Look at this number.

16,302.876

Write the **digit** that is in the hundredths place.

[ ]

_____
1 mark

10 Write these fractions in order of size, starting with the **smallest**.

$\frac{7}{12}$ $\frac{1}{6}$ $\frac{3}{4}$ $\frac{1}{4}$ $\frac{2}{3}$

[ ]   [ ]   [ ]   [ ]   [ ]

smallest

_____
2 marks

11 The length of a lesson in school is 50 minutes.
The length of the whole school day is 7.5 times the length of one lesson.

What is the length of a school day, in hours?

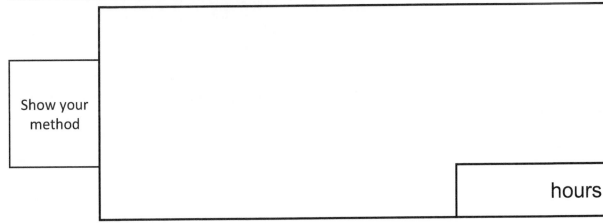

Show your method

hours

_____
3 marks

12 Brandon chooses a number less than 90.
He divides it by 4 and then takes away 7.
He then divides this result by 5.
His answer is 2.65.

What was the number he started with?

Show your
method

2 marks

13 This model is made with 25 cubes.

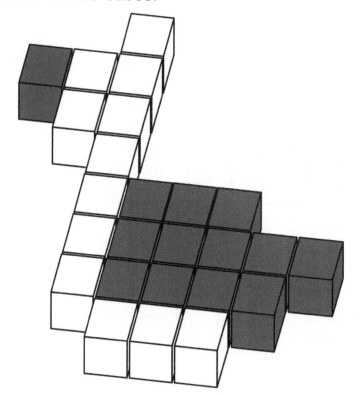

What **percentage** of the cubes in the model are black?

[ ] %

1 mark

14 Tia had a length of string.
She cut off a length of 2.7 cm.
She cut another length off of 4.8 cm.
She has two-thirds of her original string left.

$\frac{2}{3}$	4.8 cm	2.7 cm

How much string (in cm) did Tia have to start with?

Show your method

cm

3 marks

15 Lucy sells cakes at the market.

She sells $\frac{7}{16}$ of her chocolate cake.

She sells $\frac{3}{4}$ of her lemon cake.

She sells $\frac{7}{8}$ of her coffee cake.

How many cakes did she sell in total?

Show your method

cakes

2 marks

16 Siobhan buys $\frac{3}{5}$ of a piece of material.

Write the amount of material left as a percentage.

%

1 mark

17 Tania is making a patterned floor for her hallway.
She is using black and white tiles.

What percentage of the hall floor is white?

%

1 mark

18 Rufus' dad pays him £1.50 for every try that he scores in rugby.
He also pays him £1.75 for every time he gets all his spellings correct in his weekly test.
During a school term, Rufus scores 29 tries and gets all his spellings correct for 8 weeks.

How much money does his Dad have to pay Rufus at the end of term?

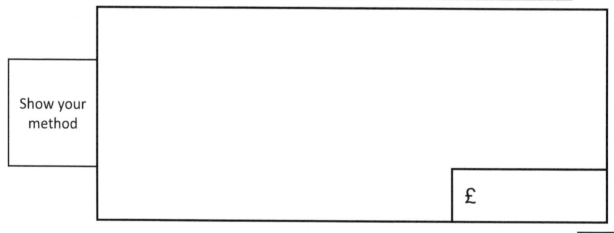

Show your method

£

3 marks

Total marks ………/30

Name _____

1 $67 \times 5 =$

1 mark

2 $\dfrac{2}{9} + \dfrac{4}{9} =$

1 mark

3 $1,567 - 100 =$

1 mark

4 $487 \times 0 =$

1 mark

5 $9 \times 4 \times 7 =$

1 mark

6 $932 + 1,000 =$

1 mark

7   965 + 707 =

1 mark

8   567 × 8 =

1 mark

9 $\frac{11}{12} - \frac{5}{12} =$

1 mark

10 $\frac{7}{8} - \frac{1}{4} =$

1 mark

11   13,298 + 5,007 =

1 mark

12   0.987 × 100 =

1 mark

13 $7^3 - 16.5 =$

1 mark

14 $\frac{9}{10} - \frac{1}{4} =$

1 mark

15 LX + IV =

1 mark

16 $\frac{3}{4} \times 4 =$

1 mark

17 $100 - 198 =$

1 mark

18 40% of £12 =

1 mark

19 $17.43 - 9.765 =$

1 mark

20 $0.45 = \dfrac{\square}{100}$

1 mark

21 $80\% = 0.\boxed{}$

1 mark

22 $376{,}095 \div 100 =$

1 mark

23 $\dfrac{1}{3} + \dfrac{1}{6} =$

1 mark

24 $189{,}067 - 99{,}109 =$

1 mark

25 L − X =

1 mark

26 $8^2 + 1.576 =$

1 mark

27 $\dfrac{2}{7} \times 6 =$

1 mark

28 $0.089 = \dfrac{}{1000}$

1 mark

29 54 ÷ 1,000 =

1 mark

30 $\dfrac{66}{100} = \boxed{}\%$

1 mark

Name _____

31 $12.6 - 9.854 =$

1 mark

32 $34{,}987 - 7{,}094 =$

1 mark

33

```
    8 4 0 3
  ×     3 6
```

Show your method   2 marks

34

```
    7 0 2 8
  ×     7 1
```

Show your method   2 marks

35

```
8 | 6 4 8 6
```

Show your method   2 marks

54

36 $5,000,000 +$ ⬚ $+ 5,000 + 60 = 5,075,060$

1 mark

37 $895,703 = 800,000 + 90,000 +$ ⬚ $+ 700 + 3$

1 mark

Total marks ………/40

1 Tick the number that is a common factor of both 15 and 20.

2   ☐

3   ☐

4   ☐

5   ☐

10   ☐

2 Here is a shape on a grid.

Complete the design so that it is symmetrical about the mirror line.

Use a ruler.

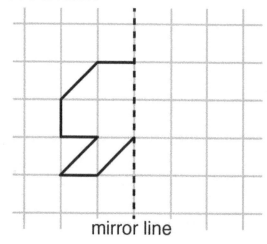

mirror line

3 The numbers in this sequence increase by the same amount each time.

Write the missing numbers.

☐   32   40   ☐   56   ☐

4 Write the missing numbers to make this **multiplication** grid correct.

×		8
	35	56
	20	

56

5 A bag of 20 potatoes costs £1.80.
A bag of 8 onions costs 96p.

How much **more** does one onion cost than one potato?

Show your method

p

2 marks

6 8 balloons cost £2.72.

4 balloons and 1 banner cost £2.08.

What is the cost of one banner?

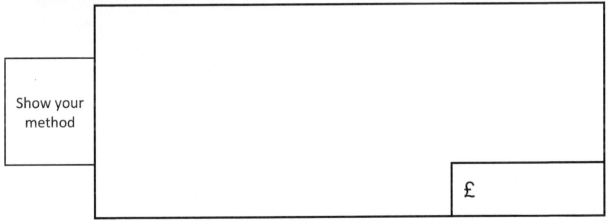

Show your method

£

2 marks

7   Here are some polygons.

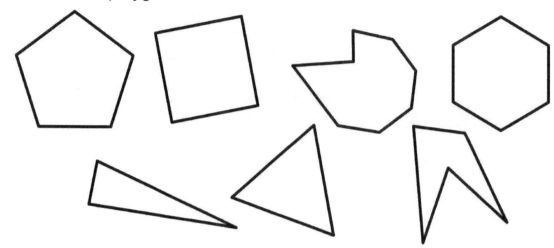

Tick all the polygons that are regular.

Explain how you know these are regular polygons.

2 marks

8   A bag contains 2.45 kg of pasta. Every Saturday, Rebecca cooks 175 g of pasta for her tea.

How many Saturdays will the bag last for?

Show your method

Saturdays

2 marks

58

9 Circle the number that is **100 times smaller** than seven hundred and sixty-four.

7,640   764   664   7.64   76,400

10 Samson and Jonah buy some football cards and stickers.

Samson buys 5 packs of 8 cards.
Jonah buys 50 single stickers for 20p each.
How much more does Jonah pay than Samson?

Pack of 8 cards

£1.55

20p each

Show your method	£

2 marks

11 Here is a net of a 3D shape.

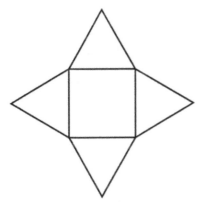

a) What is the name of the 3D shape?

b) How many vertices will the completed 3D shape have?

_____ vertices

12 In an atlas, 1 cm represents 8 km.

The distance between two towns is 320 km.

In the atlas, what is the distance between the two towns?

Show your method

cm

2 marks

13 The mass of an eraser is 12.6 g.
The mass of a pencil is half the mass
of an eraser.
The mass of a pen is 5 g more than the
mass of an eraser.

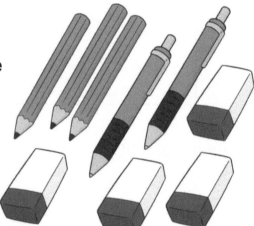

What is the **total** mass of all this
stationery?

Show your method

g

3 marks

14 Tania says,
'I put a mark on the wheel of my
bicycle and turned it until it came
back to the point. It must have
travelled 180°.'

Is she correct? Y / N

Explain your answer.

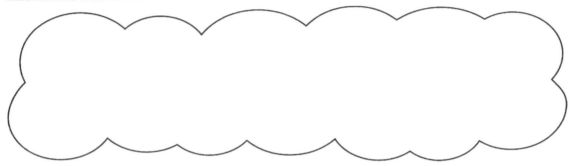

15 Two decimal numbers add together to equal 1.
One of the numbers is 0.058.

What is the other number?

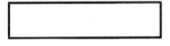

16 At a party, there are 23 guests.
There is a jug with 7 litres of squash.
Each guest pours 270 ml of squash to drink.

How much squash is left in the jug at the end?

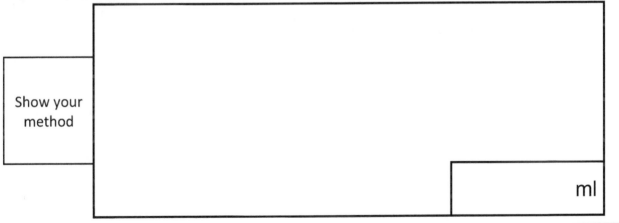

Show your
method

ml

17 Sam draws a **rectangle** on this coordinate grid.
Three of the vertices are marked.

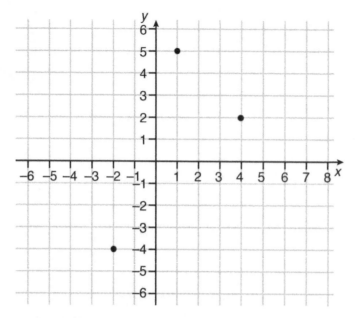

What are the coordinates of the missing vertex?

(,   )

1 mark

18 Draw a line to make an angle that is acute and mark the angle as *a*.

_____

1 mark

19 Draw an angle that is 105° and mark the angle as *b*.

_____

1 mark

20

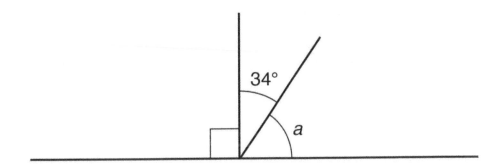

Work out angle *a*.

Show your method

°

1 mark

21

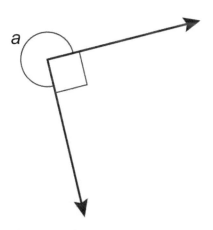

Write the value of the angle *a* that is shown here.

°

1 mark

22 A theme park has a maximum capacity of 3,968 people.
During a year, the theme park is at maximum capacity on 54 days.

How many visitors attended the park on those 54 days?

Show your method

visitors

2 marks

Total marks ..../35

1 87 − 100 =

1 mark

2 786 − 200 =

1 mark

3 85 × 8 =

1 mark

4 0.007 × 100 =

1 mark

5 829 × 7 =

1 mark

6 7 − 2.19 =

1 mark

7 $\frac{8}{13} - \frac{4}{13} =$

1 mark

8 $765 - 406 =$

1 mark

9 $9 \times 19 =$

1 mark

10 $907 \times 9 =$

1 mark

11 $70 \times 700 =$

1 mark

12 $87 \div 1{,}000 =$

1 mark

13 28.75 + 40.856 =

1 mark

14 $\frac{7}{11} - \frac{1}{2} =$

1 mark

15 69,576 + 48,794 =

1 mark

16 $\frac{6}{10} \times 7 =$

1 mark

17 LXX + XXX =

1 mark

18 $12^2 \times 2 =$

1 mark

19 $76\% = 0.\boxed{}$

1 mark

20 $\boxed{} - 8 = -15$

1 mark

21 $\dfrac{6}{13} + \dfrac{1}{2} =$

1 mark

22 $2\dfrac{3}{9} \times 6 =$

1 mark

23 $M - D =$

1 mark

24 $11^3 - 20 =$

1 mark

Name _____

25 $307.39 - 59.7 =$

1 mark

26 $1{,}471{,}067 - 996{,}598 =$

1 mark

27 $50 \times 90 =$

1 mark

28 $6\% = 0.\boxed{}$

1 mark

29 $3^2 \times 6^3 =$

1 mark

30 $605 \div 1{,}000 =$

1 mark

Name _____

31 $77\% = \dfrac{\square}{\square}$

1 mark

32 $438.31 - \boxed{} = 78.9$

1 mark

33 20% of £80 =

1 mark

34

$$
\begin{array}{r}
7\ 0\ 0\ 5 \\
\times\quad\ \ 8\ 7 \\
\hline
\end{array}
$$

Show your method   2 marks

35 8) 9 8 4 8

Show your method   2 marks

36 4) 9 0 3 7

Show your method   2 marks

37   7,906,480 = 7,000,000 + 900,000 + [   ] + 400 + 80

1 mark

Total marks ………/40

1 On the line below, mark the point that is 43 mm from point A.

A

1 mark

2 Tim puts these five numbers in their correct places on a number line.

712   789   704   756   747

a) Write the number **closest** to 750.

1 mark

b) Write the number **furthest** from 800.

1 mark

3 Mohammed uses these digit cards.

2 4 8

He makes a 2-digit number and a 1-digit number.
He multiples them together.
His answer is a **multiple of 6**.

What is Mohammed's multiplication?

☐☐ × ☐

2 marks

4 The numbers in this sequence increase by the same amount each time.
Write the missing numbers.

☐   28   53   ☐   103   ☐

2 marks

5   This diagram shows a shape that is reflected in a mirror line.

Draw the reflection of the shape in the mirror line.

Use a ruler.

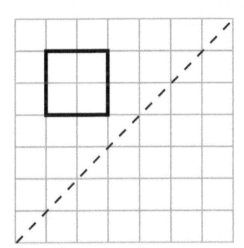

1 mark

6   Complete this table by rounding the numbers to the **nearest one hundred thousand**.

	Rounded to the nearest one hundred thousand
678,097	
358,768	
532,987	

2 marks

7   Here are four number cards.

Oscar uses each card once to make a 4-digit number.
He places:
• 9 in the tens column
• 4 so it has a higher value than any of the other digits
• the remaining two digits so that 3 has the higher value.

Write a digit in each box to show Oscar's number.

☐ ☐ ☐ ☐

1 mark

8 Lisa and Asif carry out a traffic survey on two different days.
Lisa counts 2,543 vehicles on one day.
Asif counts 1,986 vehicles on one day.

How many vehicles did they count altogether over the two days?

Show your method

vehicles

2 marks

9 Write each number in its correct place on the diagram.

89   64   2   37   81

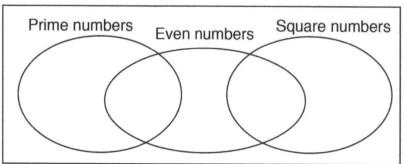

Prime numbers   Even numbers   Square numbers

2 marks

10 A box contains 4.8 kg of chicken feed.
Charlie feeds the chickens 125 grams each day.

4.8 kg

How many feeds can Charlie do?
How much is left over?

Show your method

feeds   g left over

3 marks

Name _____

11 The numbers in this sequence decrease by the same amount each time.

Write the missing numbers.

	390		210	120	

_____
2 marks

12 Complete this table by rounding the numbers to the **nearest whole number**.

	Rounded to the nearest **whole number**
0.89	
3.34	

_____
1 mark

13 Zach wants to use a mental method to calculate 286 – 92.
He starts from 286.
Here are some methods that Zach could use.

Tick the methods that are **correct**.

Add 8 then subtract 90 ☐

Subtract 100 then add 8 ☐

Subtract 2 then subtract 90 ☐

Subtract 8 then subtract 100 ☐

_____
2 marks

14 Jenny has 5 pints of milk.

Gina has $3\frac{1}{4}$ litres of milk.

1 pint = 0.57 litres

Who has the most milk? Explain your answer.

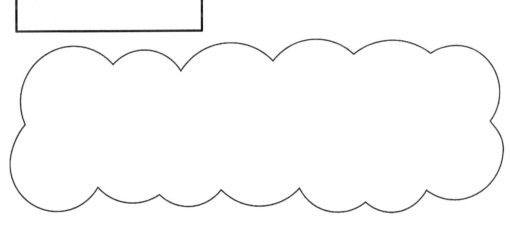

_____
1 mark

15 Nick's train journey takes 2 hours 43 minutes.
Jack's journey takes 56 minutes less than Nick's.

a) How long is Jack's journey?

hours	minutes

1 mark

Nick then takes a connecting train that he has to wait **half an hour** for.
The connecting train journey takes 75 minutes.

b) How long is Nick's complete journey, including waiting at the station?

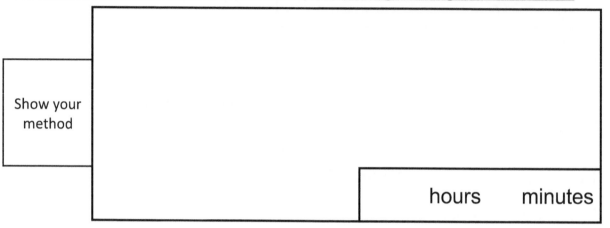

Show your method

hours	minutes

3 marks

16 Dusty makes a cuboid using 16 cubes.

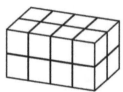

Write the letter of the cuboid that has the same volume as Dusty's cuboid.

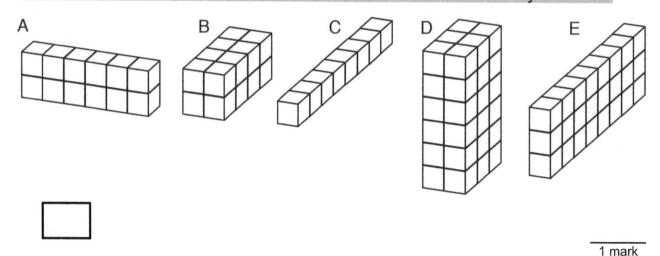

A   B   C   D   E

1 mark

17 Transform this letter by rotating it 90° **anticlockwise**.

1 mark

18 Will has to collect a stack of newspapers to deliver.
Each newspaper is 3 mm thick.
The stack has 70 newspapers in it.

a) How thick is the stack in cm?

 cm

1 mark

By 8 a.m., Will has delivered 40 newspapers.

b) How thick is the stack now in mm?

 mm

1 mark

19 A factory produces 6,754 toys.
Sandi Chain and Gina Trading
buy 1,325 each.
Sadly, 314 of the remaining toys were
broken so couldn't be sold.
John Company and Joe Shops both
buy exactly the same number of toys so
all the toys are sold.

How many toys did Joe Shops buy?

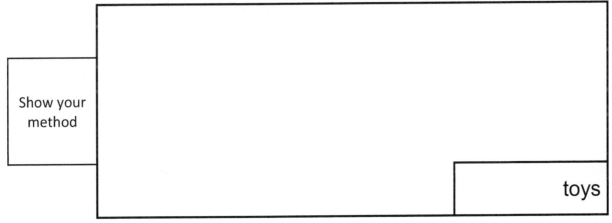

Show your method

toys

3 marks

Total marks ..../35

Year 5 Autumn Half Term 1: Arithmetic Mark Scheme

Question	Requirement	Mark	Additional guidance	Level of demand
1	795	1		T
2	685	1		T
3	767	1		T
4	6,488	1	Also accept answer written without comma.	T
5	11	1		T
6	4,605	1	Also accept answer written without comma.	T
7	7,096	1	Also accept answer written without comma.	T
8	854	1		T
9	−6	1		E
10	72	1		T
11	84	1		T
12	9,000	1	Also accept answer written without comma.	E
13	9,443	1		E
14	4,500	1	Also accept answer written without comma.	E
15	46	1		E
16	XX or 20	1		G
17	1,851	1	Also accept answer written without comma.	E
18	60	1		E
19	45	1		E
20	5,737	1	Also accept answer written without comma.	E
21	462	1		G
22	60	1		E
23	98	1		E
24	198	1		E
25	9,004	1	Also accept answer written without comma.	E
26	DCCC or 800	1		G
27	2.498	1		G
28	360,504	1		E
29	90,000	1		E
30	900,000	1		E

Threshold scores
Working towards the expected standard: 17 or fewer
Working at the expected standard: 18–23
greater depth: 24–30

Balance of difficulty of questions in the paper
10 marks at working towards (T)
16 marks at the expected standard (E)
4 marks at working at greater depth (G)

Year 5 Autumn Half Term 1: Reasoning Mark Scheme

Question	Requirement	Mark	Additional guidance	Level of demand
1	6, 5, 4 written in correct boxes	2	If incorrect, award **1 mark** for evidence of a correct method and 2 boxes correctly completed.	T
2	890	1		T
3	18 + 69 = 87	1		T
4a	7,163	1	Also accept answer written without comma.	T
4b	2,134	1	Also accept answer written without comma.	T
5	1,064 3,876 27,756	2	If incorrect, award **1 mark** for two correctly completed boxes.	T
6	23, 24	2	Do not accept any other numbers written.	T
7	755,000 755,000 750,000 800,000	3	If incorrect, award **2 marks** for 3 boxes correct **or 1 mark** for 2 boxes correct.	E
8	24°C	1		E
9	8 4 5	2	If incorrect, award **1 mark** for two boxes correctly completed.	E
10	151	1		E
11	Alphaton, Epsworth, Deltaside, Betastock, Castleby	1	Answers must be in this order for a mark.	E
12a	97 minutes	1		E
12b	17.24	1		E
13a	16 metres	1	Accept 15.5–16.5 metres.	E
13b	30 seconds	1		E
14a	£189.54	1		G
14b	£12.67	2	If incorrect, give **1 mark** for evidence of correct method with no more than 1 arithmetic error.	G

Threshold scores
Working towards the expected standard: 14 or fewer
Working at the expected standard: 15–19
Working at greater depth: 20–25

Balance of difficulty of questions in the paper
10 marks at working towards (T)
12 marks at the expected standard (E)
3 marks at working at greater depth (G)

Year 5 Autumn Half Term 2: Arithmetic Mark Scheme

Question	Requirement	Mark	Additional guidance	Level of demand
1	352	1		T
2	885	1		T
3	598	1		T
4	5,111	1	Also accept answer written without comma.	T
5	1,078	1		T
6	8,475	1	Also accept answer written without comma.	T
7	112	1		T
8	2,025	1	Also accept answer written without commas.	T
9	8,876	1	Also accept answer written without commas.	T
10	54	1		T
11	XII or 12	1		E
12	−8	1		E
13	407,994	1	Also accept answer written without comma.	E
14	5	1		G
15	65,796	1	Also accept answer written without comma.	E
16	XIII or 13	1		E
17	798,628	1	Also accept answer written without comma.	E
18	17	1		E
19	XV or 15	1		E
20	−10	1		E
21	−9	1		E
22	11,945	1	Also accept answer written without commas.	E
23	1,887,809	1	Also accept answer written without comma.	G
24	201,878	1	Also accept answer written without comma.	G
25	693,489	1	Also accept answer written without comma.	G
26	900	1		T
27	60	1		T
28	800,000	1	Also accept answer written without comma.	E
29	70,000	1	Also accept answer written without comma.	E
30	1,000	1	Also accept answer written without comma.	E

Threshold scores
Working towards the expected standard: 17 or fewer
Working at the expected standard: 18–23
Working at greater depth: 24–30

Balance of difficulty of questions in the paper
12 marks at working towards (T)
14 marks at the expected standard (E)
4 marks at working at greater depth (G)

Year 5 Autumn Half Term 2: Reasoning Mark Scheme

Question	Requirement	Mark	Additional guidance	Level of demand
1	36 wheels	1		T
2	7 6 37	2	Award **2 marks** for all three correct, award **1 mark** for 2 correct.	T
3	162 packets	2	If incorrect, award **1 mark** for evidence of a correct method.	T
4	10 cm^2	1		T
5a	7	1		T
5b	11	1		T
5c	14	1		T
6	3,640	1		E
7	36 1 2 3 4 6 9 12 18 36	3	Award **3 marks** for all 6 correct. Award **2 marks** for 4 correct. Award **1 mark** for 2 correct.	E
8a	Science	1		E
8b	1 hour 10 minutes or 70 minutes	1		E
8c	5 hours	1		E
8d	Thursday 10.20	1		E
9a	8^3	1		E
9b	512 jars	1		E
10	26.8 m	2	If incorrect, award **1 mark** for evidence of a correct method.	G
11	12 coaches	3	If incorrect, award **2 marks** for evidence of a correct method giving answer of 11.5. Award **1 mark** for evidence of a correct method with no more than one arithmetic error.	G
12	104.12m^2	1	If incorrect, award **1 mark** for evidence of a correct method with no more than one arithmetic error.	G

Threshold scores
Working towards the expected standard: 14 or fewer
Working at the expected standard: 15–19
Working at greater depth: 20–25

Balance of difficulty of questions in the paper
9 marks at working towards (T)
10 marks at the expected standard (E)
6 marks at working at greater depth (G)

Year 5 Spring Half Term 1: Arithmetic Mark Scheme

Question	Requirement	Mark	Additional guidance	Level of demand
1	224	1		T
2	$\dfrac{5}{7}$	1		T
3	824	1		T
4	1,225	1	Also accept answer written without commas.	T
5	$\dfrac{12}{8}$ or $1\dfrac{4}{8}$ or $1\dfrac{1}{2}$	1	Also accept exact decimal equivalent of 1.5.	T
6	252	1		T
7	4,422	1	Also accept answer written without commas.	T
8	$\dfrac{10}{9}$ or $1\dfrac{1}{9}$	1	Also accept exact decimal equivalent 1.1111.	T
9	12	1		T
10	XXIX or 29	1		E
11	802	1		E
12	$\dfrac{11}{12}$	1		E
13	35	1		E
14	35	1		E
15	2,665	1		E
16	900	1		E
17	$\dfrac{4}{15}$	1		E
18	9.86	1		E
19	370	1		E
20	49,000	1	Also accept answer written without commas.	E
21	M or 1,000	1		E
22	7,951	1		G
23	$\dfrac{20}{6}$ or $3\dfrac{2}{6}$ or $3\dfrac{1}{3}$	1	Also accept exact decimal equivalent 3.3333.	E
24	79.8	1		E
25	49	1		E
26	90.8	1		E
27	$\dfrac{90}{7}$ or $12\dfrac{6}{7}$	1		E
28	800	1		E
29	4,867	1		G
30	$\dfrac{61}{28}$ or $2\dfrac{5}{28}$	1		G
31	25,785	2	Award **2 marks** for the correct answer of **25,785**. If the answer is incorrect, award **1 mark** for a formal method of long multiplication with no more than 1 arithmetic error.	G

| 32 | 832 | 2 | Award **2 marks** for the correct answer of **832**. If the answer is incorrect, award **1 mark** for a formal method of division with no more than 1 arithmetic error. | G |
| 33 | 9,000 | 1 | Also accept answer written without commas. | E |

Threshold scores
Working towards the expected standard: 20 or fewer
Working at the expected standard: 21–27
Working at greater depth: 28–35

Balance of difficulty of questions in the paper
9 marks working towards the expected standard (T)
19 marks working at the expected standard (E)
7 marks working at greater depth (G)

Year 5 Spring Half Term 1: Reasoning Mark Scheme

Question	Requirement	Mark	Additional guidance	Level of demand
1	36	1		T
2	9	1		T
3	$\frac{1}{4}, \frac{1}{3}, \frac{1}{2}, \frac{3}{4}, \frac{9}{16}$	2	If incorrect, award **1 mark** for 3 correctly matched.	T
4	0.75 and $\frac{75}{100}$ ticked	1	Do not award the mark if any other boxes are ticked.	T
5	100	1		E
6	$\frac{4}{5}$ $\frac{56}{70}$	2	Award **1 mark** for each correct answer up to a maximum of two.	E
7	Explanation should show that it is correct but no mark to be given for just circling Y.	2	**1 mark** for evidence of showing that $\frac{8}{8} + \frac{8}{8} + \frac{4}{8} = \frac{20}{8}$ 1 mark for explaining that $\frac{4}{8}$ is equivalent to $\frac{1}{2}$	E
8	$\frac{2}{3}$ or any fraction equivalent to $\frac{2}{3}$	2	If incorrect, award **1 mark** for evidence of a correct method with no more than one arithmetic error.	E
9	$8\frac{1}{8}$	2	If incorrect, award **1 mark** for evidence of $\frac{65}{8}$ but error in converting to a mixed number.	E
10	In order: 0.25, 0.8, 0.016, 0.4	2	If incorrect, award **1 mark** for 2 correctly matched.	E
11	6	2	If incorrect, award **1 mark** for evidence of a correct method with no more than one arithmetic error.	E
12	2018	1		E
13	34 boxes	3	If incorrect, award **2 marks** for evidence of a correct method and sight of the calculation 204 ÷ 6. Award **1 mark** for evidence of a correct method for the multiplications.	G
14	$\frac{1}{5} < \frac{1}{4} < \frac{1}{2} < \frac{9}{10}$	1	Any three chosen but written in the order shown here.	E
15	2 3	3	If incorrect, award **2 marks** for 1 correct box. Award **1 mark** for a correct method with only 1 arithmetic error.	G
16a	23 chocolates in each box	1		G
16b	4 left over	1		G
17a	95,370	1		E
17b	95,000	1		E

Year 5 Spring Half Term 1: Reasoning Mark Scheme

Threshold scores
Working towards the expected standard: 17 or fewer
Working at the expected standard: 18–23
Working at greater depth: 24–30

Balance of difficulty of questions in the paper
5 marks at working towards (T)
17 marks at the expected standard (E)
8 marks at working at greater depth (G)

Year 5 Spring Half Term 2: Arithmetic Mark Scheme

Question	Requirement	Mark	Additional guidance	Level of demand
1	494	1		T
2	$\frac{5}{9}$	1	Also accept exact decimal equivalent 0.555.	T
3	1,153	1	Also accept answer written without comma.	T
4	9,679	1	Also accept answer written without comma.	T
5	4,376	1	Also accept answer written without comma.	T
6	40	1		T
7	3.68	1		T
8	$\frac{5}{12}$	1		T
9	25 0r 0.25	1		T
10	2.96	1		T
11	£19.36	1		T
12	16,800	1		E
13	−100	1		E
14	75	1		E
15	86	1		E
16	$\frac{8}{7}$ or $1\frac{1}{7}$	1		E
17	0.124	1		E
18	$\frac{11}{10}$ or $1\frac{1}{10}$	1	Also accept exact decimal equivalent 1.1.	E
19	8	1		E
20	7.54	1		E
21	0.054	1		E
22	27	1		E
23	$\frac{3}{10}$	1		E
24	100	1		E
25	32	1		E
26	$\frac{10}{4}$ or $2\frac{2}{4}$ or $2\frac{1}{2}$	1		E
27	$\frac{16}{30}$ or $\frac{8}{15}$	1	Also accept exact decimal equivalent 0.5333.	E
28	84.36	1		E
29	142.56	1		G
30	$\frac{104}{6}$ or $17\frac{2}{6}$ or $17\frac{1}{3}$	1	Also accept exact decimal equivalent 17.333.	G

31	$\frac{19}{15}$ or $1\frac{4}{15}$	1		G
32	42,804	2	Award **2 marks** for the correct answer of **42,804**. If the answer is incorrect, award **1 mark** for a formal method of long multiplication with no more than 1 arithmetic error.	G
33	1340.5	2	Award **2 marks** for the correct answer of **1340.5**. If the answer is incorrect, award **1 mark** for a formal method of division with no more than 1 arithmetic error.	G

Threshold scores
Working towards the expected standard: 20 or fewer
Working at the expected standard: 21–27
Working at greater depth: 28–35

Balance of difficulty of questions in the paper
11 marks working towards the expected standard (T)
17 marks working at the expected standard (E)
7 marks working at greater depth (G)

Year 5 Spring Half Term 2: Reasoning Mark Scheme

Question	Requirement	Mark	Additional guidance	Level of demand
1	70,600	1		T
2	306 stickers	2	If incorrect, award **1 mark** for evidence of correct method with no more than one arithmetic error.	T
3	74 × 9	1		T
4	$\dfrac{2}{8}$ $\dfrac{3}{12}$	1		T
5	1,500 km	2	If incorrect, award **1 mark** for evidence of a correct method with no more than 1 arithmetic error.	T
6	£8.55	2	If incorrect, award **1 mark** for evidence of a correct method with no more than 1 arithmetic error.	T
7	$\dfrac{52}{9}$	1		E
8	0.54, 0.687, 2.08, 2.8	1		E
9	7	1		E
10	$\dfrac{1}{6}, \dfrac{1}{4}, \dfrac{7}{12}, \dfrac{2}{3}, \dfrac{3}{4}$	2	If incorrect, award **1 mark** for 3 correctly ordered.	E
11	6.25 hours or $6\dfrac{1}{4}$ hours	3	If incorrect, award **2 marks** for correct answer given in minutes but incorrectly converted to hours. Award **1 mark** for evidence of correct method with no more than one arithmetic error.	G
12	81	2	If incorrect, award **1 mark** for evidence of a correct method with no more than 1 arithmetic error.	E
13	52%	1		E
14	22.5 cm	3	If incorrect, award **2 marks** for evidence of correct method and clear answer of 7.5 cm shown as the amount taken off with evidence of multiplying this by 3. Award **1 mark** for evidence of correct method with no more than one arithmetic error.	G
15	$\dfrac{33}{16}$ or $2\dfrac{1}{16}$	2	If incorrect, award **1 mark** for evidence of a correct method.	G
16	40%	1		E
17	64%	1		E
18	£57.50	3	If incorrect, award **2 marks** for evidence of correct method with no more than one arithmetic error. Award **1 mark** for evidence of correct method but more than one error.	G

Threshold scores
Working towards the expected standard: 17 or fewer
Working at the expected standard: 18–23
Working at greater depth: 24–30

Balance of difficulty of questions in the paper
9 marks at working towards (T)
10 marks at the expected standard (E)
11 marks at working at greater depth (G)

Year 5 Summer Half Term 1: Arithmetic Mark Scheme

Question	Requirement	Mark	Additional guidance	Level of demand
1	335	1		T
2	$\frac{6}{9}$ or $\frac{2}{3}$	1		T
3	1,467	1	Also accept answer written without comma.	T
4	0	1		T
5	252	1		T
6	1,932	1	Also accept answer written without comma.	T
7	1,672	1	Also accept answer written without comma.	T
8	4,536	1	Also accept answer written without comma.	T
9	$\frac{6}{12}$ or $\frac{1}{2}$	1	Also accept exact decimal equivalent 0.5.	T
10	$\frac{5}{8}$	1	Also accept exact decimal equivalent 0.625.	T
11	18,305	1	Also accept answer written without comma.	E
12	98.7	1		E
13	326.5	1		E
14	$\frac{13}{20}$	1	Also accept exact decimal equivalent 0.65.	E
15	LXIV or 64	1		E
16	3	1		E
17	−98	1		E
18	£4.80	1		E
19	7.665	1		E
20	45	1		E
21	0.8	1		E
22	3760.95	1		E
23	$\frac{3}{6}$ or $\frac{1}{2}$ or equivalent	1	Also accept exact decimal equivalent 0.5.	E
24	89,958	1		E
25	XL or 40	1		E
26	65.576	1		E
27	$\frac{12}{7}$ or $1\frac{5}{7}$	1	Also accept exact decimal equivalent 1.714…	G
28	$\frac{89}{1000}$	1		E
29	0.054	1		E
30	66%	1		E
31	2.746	1		G
32	27,893	1		G

Year 5 Summer Half Term 1: Arithmetic Mark Scheme

33	302,508	2	Award **2 marks** for the correct answer of **302,508**. If the answer is incorrect, award **1 mark** for a formal method of long multiplication with no more than 1 arithmetic error.	G
34	498,988	2	Award **2 marks** for the correct answer of **498,988**. If the answer is incorrect, award **1 mark** for a formal method of long multiplication with no more than 1 arithmetic error.	G
35	810.75	2	Award **2 marks** for the correct answer of **810.75**. If the answer is incorrect, award **1 mark** for a formal method of division with no more than 1 arithmetic error.	G
36	70,000	1	Also accept answer written without comma.	E
37	5,000	1	Also accept answer written without comma.	E

Threshold scores
Working towards the expected standard: 23 or fewer
Working at the expected standard: 24–31
Working at greater depth: 32–40

Balance of difficulty of questions in the paper
10 marks working towards the expected standard (T)
21 marks working at the expected standard (E)
9 marks working at greater depth (G)

Year 5 Summer Half Term 1: Reasoning Mark Scheme

Question	Requirement	Mark	Additional guidance	Level of demand
1	5	1		T
2		1		T
3	24, 48, 64	1		E
4	<table><tr><td>×</td><td>**5**</td><td>8</td></tr><tr><td>**7**</td><td>35</td><td>56</td></tr><tr><td>**4**</td><td>20</td><td>**32**</td></tr></table>	2	If incorrect, award **1 mark** for 2 boxes correctly completed.	T
5	3p	2	If incorrect, award **1 mark** for evidence of a correct method but no more than one arithmetic error.	T
6	£0.72 or 72p	2	If incorrect, award **1 mark** for evidence of a correct method but no more than one arithmetic error.	T
7		2	If incorrect, award **1 mark** for 2 correctly identified and no incorrect ones identified.	E
8	14	2	If incorrect, award **1 mark** for evidence of a correct method but no more than one arithmetic error.	E
9	7.64	1		E
10	£2.25	2	If incorrect, award **1 mark** for evidence of a correct method but no more than one arithmetic error.	E
11a	Square-based pyramid	1	Spelling does not need to be correct for the award of the mark.	E
11b	5	1		E
12	40 cm	2	If incorrect, award **1 mark** for evidence of a correct method but no more than one arithmetic error.	E
13	104.5 g	3	If incorrect, award **2 marks** for evidence of correct mass of each item and method with correct multiplication. Award **1 mark** for evidence of a correct method but more than one arithmetic error.	G
14	N: Explanation should show that it is incorrect as it has travelled a full turn which is 360°	1	Award of mark can be given if explanation correct but N not circled. N alone circled is not acceptable for the mark.	E
15	0.942	1		E
16	790ml or 0.79 L	3	If incorrect, award **2 marks** for evidence of method with correct multiplication. Award **1 mark** for evidence of a correct method but more than one arithmetic error.	G
17	(−5, −1)	1		E
18	Line drawn from one end of line to make an angle that is less than 90 degrees.	1		E
19	Check angle is 105°	1	Allow error of 1° either side.	E

20	56°	1		E
21	270°	1		E
22	214,272	2	If incorrect, award **1 mark** for evidence of method with correct multiplication.	G

Threshold scores
Working towards the expected standard: 20 or fewer
Working at the expected standard: 21–27
Working at greater depth: 28–35

Balance of difficulty of questions in the paper
8 marks at working towards (T)
19 marks at the expected standard (E)
8 marks at working at greater depth (G)

Year 5 Summer Half Term 2: Arithmetic Mark Scheme

Question	Requirement	Mark	Additional guidance	Level of demand
1	−13	1		T
2	586	1		T
3	680	1		T
4	0.7	1		T
5	5,803	1	Also accept answer written without comma.	T
6	4.81	1		T
7	$\frac{4}{13}$	1		T
8	359	1		T
9	171	1		T
10	8,163	1	Also accept answer written without comma.	T
11	49,000	1	Also accept answer written without comma.	E
12	0.087	1		E
13	69.606	1		E
14	$\frac{3}{22}$	1		E
15	118,370	1	Also accept answer written without comma.	E
16	$\frac{42}{10}$ or $4\frac{1}{5}$ or 4.2 or equivalent	1		E
17	C or 100	1		E
18	288	1		E
19	0.76	1		E
20	−7	1		E
21	$\frac{25}{26}$	1		E
22	$\frac{126}{9}$ or 14 or equivalent	1		G
23	D or 500	1		E
24	1,311	1	Also accept answer written without comma.	E
25	247.69	1		E
26	474,469	1	Also accept answer written without comma.	G
27	4,500	1	Also accept answer written without comma.	E
28	0.06	1		E
29	1,944	1	Also accept answer written without comma.	G
30	0.605	1		E
31	$\frac{77}{100}$ or equivalent	1		E
32	359.41	1		E

33	£16	1		G
34	609,435	2	Award **2 marks** for the correct answer of **609,435**. If the answer is incorrect, award **1 mark** for a formal method of long multiplication with no more than 1 arithmetic error.	G
35	1,231	2	Award **2 marks** for the correct answer of **1,231**. If the answer is incorrect, award **1 mark** for a formal method of division with no more than 1 arithmetic error.	G
36	2,259.25	2	Award **2 marks** for the correct answer of **2,259.25**. If the answer is incorrect, award **1 mark** for a formal method of division with no more than 1 arithmetic error.	G
37	6,000	1	Also accept answer written without comma.	E

Threshold scores
Working towards the expected standard: 23 or fewer
Working at the expected standard: 24–31
Working at greater depth: 32–40

Balance of difficulty of questions in the paper
10 marks working towards the expected standard (T)
20 marks working at the expected standard (E)
10 marks working at greater depth (G)

Year 5 Summer Half Term 2: Reasoning Mark Scheme

Question	Requirement	Mark	Additional guidance	Level of demand
1	Check child's measurement is 43 mm away from point A	1	Allow ± 1 mm	T
2a	747	1		T
2b	704	1		T
3	48 x 2 or 84 x 2 or 24 x 8 or 42 x 8	2	If incorrect, evidence of trial and error and multiplications but not one selected for **1 mark**.	T
4	3, 78, 128	2	If incorrect, award **1 mark** for 2 correctly completed boxes.	T
5		1		T
6	700,000 400,000 500,000	2	Award **1 mark** for 2 correct.	E
7	4398	1		E
8	4,529	2	If incorrect, award **1 mark** for evidence of a correct method.	E
9		2	Award **1 mark** for 3 correctly placed.	E
10	38 feeds 50 g left over	3	Award **2 marks** for evidence of a correct method and answer but incorrect amount left over. Award **1 mark** for evidence of a correct method but with more than one arithmetic error.	G
11	480, 300, 30	2	If incorrect, award **1 mark** for 2 correctly completed boxes.	E
12	1 3	1		E
13	Subtract 100 then add 8 Subtract 2 then subtract 90	2	Award **1 mark** for 1 correctly identified with no incorrect ticks.	E
14	Gina as she has 3,250 ml and Jenny only has 2,850 ml	1		G
15a	1 hour 47 minutes or equivalent	1		E
15b	4 hours 28 minutes or equivalent	3	If incorrect, award **2 marks** for evidence of correct method but no conversion to hours and minutes. Award **1 mark** for evidence of a correct method but with more than one arithmetic error.	G
16	B	1		E
17		1		G
18a	21 cm	1		E
18b	90 mm	1		E

19	1,895		3	If incorrect, award **2 marks** for evidence of correct method and each step identified but one arithmetic error.	G
				Award **1 mark** for evidence of a correct method but with more than one arithmetic error.	

Threshold scores
Working towards the expected standard: 20 or fewer
Working at the expected standard: 21–27
Working at greater depth: 28–35

Balance of difficulty of questions in the paper
8 marks at working towards (T)
16 marks at the expected standard (E)
11 marks at working at greater depth (G)

Content domain references

Autumn 1: Arithmetic	
Question	Content domain ref.
1	3C2
2	3C1/3M2b
3	3N2b
4	4C2
5	4N2b
6	4C2
7	4N1
8	4N3a
9	4C2
10	4N2b
11	4N1
12	4N3a
13	5N5/5N6
14	5N1/3N2b
15	5N3a/5N6
16	5N5/5N6
17	5C2
18	5N3b/5N6
19	5N3a/5N6
20	5N1/3N2b
21	5N5/5N6
22	5N3b/5N6
23	5N5/5N6
24	5C2
25	5C2
26	5C2
27	5C2
28	5N3b/5N6
29	5N3a/5N6
30	5N5/5N6

Autumn 1: Reasoning	
Question	Content domain ref.
1	3C2
2	3N2b
3a	3C3
4a	4S1/5C2
4b	4S1/5C2
5	4N2b
6	4N6
7	5N4
8	5N5
9	5N3a
10	5N3b
11	5N2
12a	5S1
12b	5S1
13	5S2
14	5C4

Autumn 2: Arithmetic	
Question	Content domain ref.
1	3N2b
2	3C2
3	3C2
4	4C2
5	4C6a
6	4C2
7	4N2b
8	5N5/5N6
9	4C6a
10	4C6b
11	5N3a/5N6
12	5C2
13	5C6a
14	5N3b/5N6
15	5C2
16	5C6a
17	5C2
18	5C5d
19	5C6a
20	5C6b
21	5N3a/5N6
22	5C6b
23	5C2
24	5N3b/5N6
25	5C6b
26	4C6b
27	5C6b
28	5N3a/5N6
29	5C5d
30	5C5d

Autumn 2: Reasoning	
Question	Content domain ref.
1	3C8
2	3S2
3	4C8/4C7
4	4M7b
5	4S2
6	5C6b
7	5C5a
8a	5S1
8b	5S1
8c	5S1
8d	5S1
9	5C5d
10	5M7a
11	5C8a
12	5M7b/5C7a

Content domain references

Spring 1: Arithmetic

Question	Content domain ref.
1	3C7
2	3F4
3	3C2
4	4C7
5	4F4
6	4C6b
7	4C7
8	4F4
9	4C6a
10	5N3b
11	5C6b
12	5F4
13	5N5/5N6
14	5F5
15	5C2
16	5C6a
17	5F4
18	5C6b
19	5C5d
20	5C6a
21	5N3b
22	5C2
23	5F5
24	5C6b
25	5C5d
26	5C6b
27	5F5
28	5C6a
29	5C2
30	5F4
31	5C7a
32	5C7b
33	5N3a

Spring 1: Reasoning

Question	Content domain ref.
1	3C7
2	3C8
3	4F2
4	4F6a/4F6b
5	5C6b
6	5F2b
7	5F2a
8	5F4
9	5F5
10	5F6a

Question	Content domain ref.
11	5C8c
12	5N3b
13	5C8a/5C7a/5C7b
14	5F3
15	5C7a
16	5C7b
17a	5N4
17b	5N4

Spring 2: Arithmetic

Question	Content domain ref.
1	3C2
2	3F4
3	3C2
4	4N2b
5	4C7
6	4F6b
7	4F8
8	4F4
9	4F6a
10	4F8
11	4F10b
12	5C2
13	5N5
14	5F11
15	5F6a
16	5F2a/4F4
17	5F8
18	5F4
19	5F2b
20	5F10
21	5F6b
22	5F5
23	5F11
24	5F6a
25	5F2b
26	5F2a/4F4
27	5F4
28	5F10
29	5C5d
30	5F5
31	5F4
32	5C7a
33	5C7b

Spring 2: Reasoning

Question	Content domain ref.
1	3C8
2	3C8, 3C6
3	4C8
4	4F2
5	4F10a
6	4F10b
7	5F2a
8	5F8
9	5F6b
10	5F3
11	5F5
12	5F10
13	5F12
14	5F10
15	5F4
16	5F6a
17	5F11
18	5C8c

Content domain references

Summer 1: Arithmetic

Question	Content domain ref.
1	3C7
2	3F4
3	3N2b
4	4C6b
5	4C6b
6	4N2b
7	4C2
8	4C7
9	4F4
10	5F4
11	5C2
12	5C6b
13	5C5d
14	5F4
15	5N3b
16	5F5
17	5N5
18	5N3b
19	5F10
20	5F6a
21	5F11
22	5C6b
23	5F4
24	5C2
25	5N3b
26	5C5d
27	5F5
28	5F6b
29	5C6b
30	5F11
31	5F10
32	5C2
33	5C7a
34	5C7a
35	5C7b
36	5N3a
37	5N3a

Summer 1: Reasoning

Question	Content domain ref.
1	3M9a
2	3M9a/4F10b
3	4G2c
4	4C6a
5	4F10b
6	5G2b
7	5M9c
8	5C6b
9	5M9a
10	5G3b
11	5M9b
12	5M9c
13	5G4b
14	5C6a
15	5F10
16	5M9d, 5M5
17	5G2a
18	5G4a
19	5G4c
20	5G4b
21	5G4b
22	5C7a

Summer 2: Arithmetic

Question	Content domain ref.
1	3N2b/4N5
2	3C1
3	3C7
4	4C6b
5	4C7
6	4F8
7	4F4
8	4C2
9	4C6a
10	4C7
11	5C6a
12	5C6b
13	5F8
14	5F4
15	5C2
16	5F5
17	5N3b
18	5C5d
19	5F11
20	5N5
21	5F4

Question	Content domain ref.
22	5F5
23	5N3b
24	5C5d
25	5F8
26	5C2
27	5C6a
28	5F11
29	5C5d/4C7
30	5C6b
31	5F11
32	5F8
33	5C2
34	5C7a
35	5C7b
36	5C7b
37	5N3a

Summer 2: Reasoning

Question	Content domain ref.
1	3M2a
2a	3N2a
2b	3N2a
3	4C8
4	4N1
5	4G2c
6	5N4
7	5N3a
8	5C2
9	5C5c/5C5b
10	5M5/5C8a
11	5N1
12	5F7
13	5C1
14	5M6
15a	5M4
15b	5M4
16	5M8
17	5P2
18a	5M9d
18b	5M9d
19	5C8b

Name _____   Class _____

Year 5/P6 Maths Progress Tests for White Rose Record Sheet

Tests	Mark	Total marks	Key skills to target
Autumn 1: Arithmetic			
Autumn 1: Reasoning			
Autumn 2: Arithmetic			
Autumn 2: Reasoning			
Spring 1: Arithmetic			
Spring 1: Reasoning			
Spring 2: Arithmetic			
Spring 2: Reasoning			
Summer 1: Arithmetic			
Summer 1: Reasoning			
Summer 2: Arithmetic			
Summer 2: Reasoning			